Ocean of Emotions

Aditi Chandrasekhar

BlueRose ONE .com DIY
Stories Matter

Published by: BlueRose Publishers

Address: B-6, Amaltash Marg, Block B, Sector 4, Noida, Uttar Pradesh 201301
Email: info@bluerosepublishers.com
Website: BlueRoseONE.com

Cover design and illustrations by: Ranjitha M C

ISBN: 978-93-5628-821-8

Printed by: BlueRose Publishers

Dedication

This book is dedicated to my wonderful family, my friends, and my mentors

Contents

Foreword

It is a joy and sublime experience to write a foreword to Ms. Aditi Chandrasekhar's verses composed over a period. The poetic compositions are beautiful reflection of Aditi's heart, mind and eloquent expression in verse. A teenager, a high school senior, in fact has composed in poetry such profound and sensitive expression of human feelings and sensibilities, most admirable in beauty, power, and emotive reflections of deep human thoughts, experiences in vocabulary and verse. It is an amazing mirror to Aditi's endowments in thought and creative expression, hallmarks of a budding poet.

Almost every poem in the collection touches the readers in their heart, reality of life's experiences at a movingly deep level. The collection of verses in their theme and narrative, touch everyone in their lives. Several of the experiences common in their lives, we can expect from Aditi in future, eloquent, moving works of beauty, sublime feelings soulful and stirring in verse and compositions. I wish her ever good future in these expressions of this rare talent, most strikingly so much part of her heart and thoughts.

Bangalore
June 5, 2022

Rukmini Krishnaswamy
Technical Director
Spastics Society of Karnataka

Preface

The many thoughts coursing through me needed an outlet and I was inspired to write poetry at a very young age. I present to you my 'Oceans of Emotions'.

Anger

Anger an art, an emotion
may not be one's best friend
but surely can be made one's best friend
Emotions may come out in the form of anger
Anger may come out in the form of emotions

Anger is beautiful
and can sometimes
be as strong as the winds
but it never dies

Anger may be that
one thing which can be handled better
Art and emotions
can add color and
can help discover new buddies

Anger an art
a true best friend
an emotion
wonderful companion

Aspirations

Sleepless nights
Restless days
Individuals may face

Daring ambitions
Fighting odds
With time and space

Brain cells
Knocking one's door
As pursuits hit one for sure

Imaginations running wild
Like individuals who cried
Dreams possible to achieve
as screams possible to receive

Aspiring magnanimous desires
Fulfilled by one
Despairing generous inclination
Followed by none

Autism

Beautiful bonds
Created one
Misunderstood by everyone

Feeling sympathetic
for some
but empathetic for none

Fears chasing
around one's brain
tracks creaking as noise of train

Cries of none
Like in darkness
Skies of none that brightens

Anxiety seen in eyes of one
Anger heard
in cries of some

Beautiful bonds
unknown
wonderful bonds unbroken

Beautiful bonds
never dies
no worries, no more cries

Birds of paradise

Birds of paradise
The love of two souls
Folk together as one
These beaks and feathers

always there to guide and watch
The two birds were never near
They were always on the fly
The very next thing that happens
the hearts became one

The souls merged together
Soar to great heights
Never let your wings down
Soar to great levels
Never let your wings break

You've opened a door
You've opened your hearts
The joy and love, passion and emotion
Defines the birds

The harmonious sounds that you create
Can't express love
But nothing of this matter
when it comes to love

Soar to great heights
Never let your wings down
Soar to great levels
Never let your wings break

The love of two souls
Folk together as one
These beaks and feathers
Are always there to guide and watch

Breeze on my skin

Trails of nature
all around
that feature
beauty that surround
Nature can be frail
but beauty never fails.

Call from the winds
that create
sounds pleasant to ears
chirps from heaven
that pass by
the years

Flight of the breeze
that touches individual's skin
and watch horizons grin
What a sight you
say in woah a bright shine
we say we saw

Trails that nature
all around
that feature beauty
that surround
Nature can be frail
but beauty never fails.

Butterflies of life

Look at the vast skies above and the stringy rain
Look at the pushy green leaves and the strips of torn leaves
The colors come together and form some beautiful designs
The hand looms are the same, they come together and reunite

Looms after looms keep curling up like lil caterpillars
that later go and weave the color and become butterflies
Looms are very beautifully created
Cause they are compared to the four stages of life

The gay blue color represents the birth of the newborn
The dark red and orange color speak about the sunset
The black and white compares to many symbolic indications
They are beautiful created and compared to life's first cry and the last breath

Looms after looms keep curling up like lil caterpillars
that later go and weave the color and become butterflies
Look at the vast skies above
And the stringy rain

Look at the pushy green leaves and the strips of torn leaves
The colors come together and form some beautiful designs
The hand looms are the same
They come together and reunite

Dearly tear

Ever since I met you, you just stole my heart
We just could not be parted ever

My heart feels wounded right now because you are not here with me
Seeing everyone having grandfathers it makes my heart just sink unbearably

Wonderful person you left us, and we will still keep you in our hearts
But if you ever return, our hearts will become joyful again

The first time I saw you, you just made me feel the person that I am and you made me realise my worth. You have and will always be my number one supporter

I love you.

Wonderful person you left us, but we will still keep you in our hearts
But if you ever return, our hearts will become joyful again.

Whenever you were near me, the waves that you had spread really made me feel that I knew and I could count on you

Amazing person you left us, but we still keep you in our hearts
But if you ever return, our hearts will become joyful again.

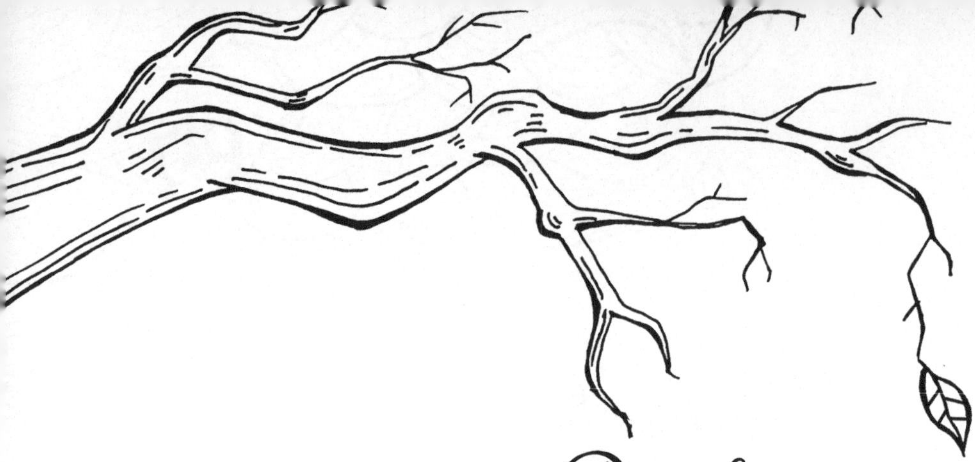

Death

Death is a very graceful moment in life

If you ever received love from a person
who is not with you, Cherish it

Death brings loss of emotions and pearls
To the ones that are left behind

This is the period that people get intrigued
And there is a sense of folks wanting to know the cause.

Many a time
we don't realise the value of something
Unless made a memory

Most of the time
people want to know everything
the folks that are left behind often shed pearls.

Death is a very graceful moment in life

If you ever received love from a person
who is not with you, Cherish it.

Decorate your agony

We all go through that one phase
when we think that everything
has gone south
There are ways to overcome that

We as humans need to believe in ourselves
we need to recreate
a whole new world for us
and the peninsulas around us.

Our agonies may not be that bad
but we don't realize If we ever have any type of friends
or even any relationship with people
that take their pain in their stride
we then would truly know whose agony is more.

Decorate your agony doesn't mean that you
should add designs to it
but it means that we should bring out emotions
that one has in the form of art.

We may all go through
these phase of life without understanding that
this is how life unfolds

Desolation

Depression found in one's faces smile
Agony bottled up inside

Desolation, an emotion not be easy
For some daunting to stop the run

Captured to one's throat
Like horses to reign

Enhancing sunshine
Like conquering of rains

Standstill occurs everywhere
Desolation too

Destiny

Fears of losing someone may suddenly occur
and that makes one suffer
Peers may appear in many ways
and can also part along within days

Written not written why bother when
miracles may come thy way
Bitten, not fitting in, how does it matter when
you can be like the breeze that sways

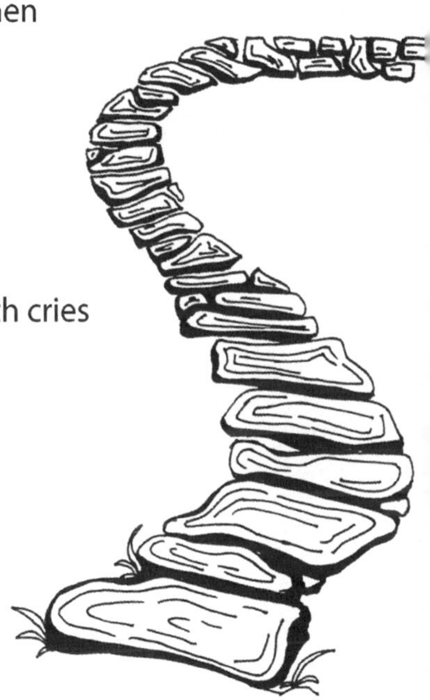

Why fear or pain when
the sphere around don't fade or die
Why a derived sense of gain
just to achieve something pale and show it with cries

Individuals are beautiful pieces
what need to change
Life will not hold sway over your day
walk with rains and smile through pains

Huge dusty depths to walk through
Some bushes may sometimes be ferocious
but unknown to the human race support rains
down like smiles hidden behind the simple face

Plans nipped in the bud through inaction
And moments lost in a fraction
The human race has long stakes
And memories built through millennia

Fathers and daughters

A father and daughter share a special bond
But when a father must leave his daughter
it feels like the bond is broken

The father may have to go on trips for maybe
days together or just a few days
But for most of the daughters it may sometimes it hard

This bond should not be
taken advantage of
But it should be cherished

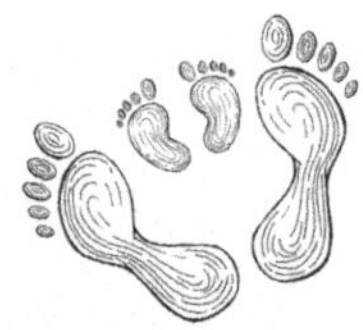

The relationship between a father and a daughter
should not only be felt at the time of saying a final goodbye
or at the time of marriage.

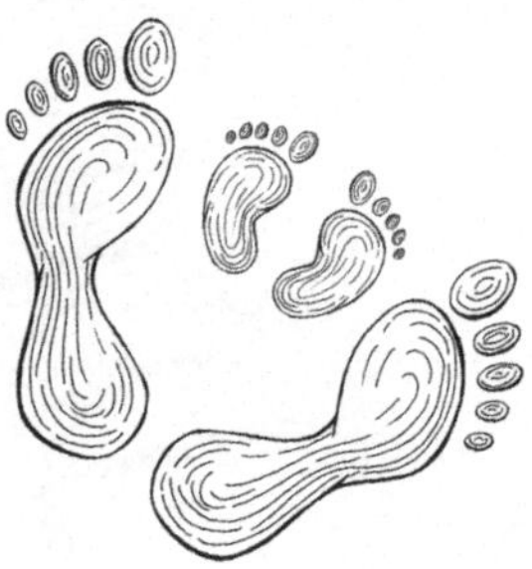

The bonds that the father and daughter
share will always be a part
of both the souls.

Every time a father must say a bye, it's hard
But when it comes to a daughter waving a bye
it puts the smile on the father's face.

A father and daughter share a special bond
But when a father must leave his daughter,
it feels like the bond is broken.

Flames of wild skies

Tiny sparks fly high
Oh! what sigh
Dust to ashes
Branches shaped in ashes

Trees that high five
constellations that thrive
beauty in everything
one may see

Cold winter skies
In one's embers eyes
Wonders that one may feel
in their cries

Flowers of the forest

Flowers of the forest, that's you and I
We shine in the sunlight, then fade and die
Too many hearts broken all the way
Too many girls left at break of day
If you could see in me, what would you say?
God give me the strength for I am leaving today
Another heartbroken all the way
Another young flower trampled away

Friendship I

Friendships come and friendships goes around the world
We make up and we break up
and the friendship comes back again
Friendships come and friendships goes around the world
We make up and we break up
But friendship never dies

Friendship II

Friendship is an amazing relationship in life
Because friendship gives you privacy
and makes you share experience and encourage each other

True friendship is that one
relationship which will never die
Friendship should continue forever

Gold coins never fall

You may have a rough day
You may have a challenging time
But don't let there
be a moment that makes
You drift apart from the person you love
And the person who loves you.

People say that silence is golden
But no, it's not always golden
Every individual may
have their own judgements
They need to know that
it can be hard for them once anything is in the open.

Mankind can also
be very tricky with its nature
But we need to have
The courage to
face and overcome
the pain that we have created for ourselves.

You may have a rough day
You may have a challenging time
But don't let there
be a moment that makes you
drift apart from the person you love
And the person who loves you.

Hardships

Sails through rough oceans
Tides high and low
Canvas of notions
Paint and show

Summons may arouse
feelings not so good
Tiger's mood may induce
as it triggers like it should

Ships with yachts
flying at mast
Dares that hatch
from the past

One's dream may grow
As trees may sow

Hearts

Friendship that never dies
Beauty stays strong
Voices that cry
One's love prolong

Cares of emotion
Caress one's heart
Hearts of bears
Hug out one's passion

Always beating to glory
Soaring to trust
Never stopes respiring
Always feels sorry

Jealousy

Resentment seen in one
like cold winds for none

Soaring birds up in skies
like weaving of heavens that lies

Aspirations getting lost with cries
inspirations getting won like fries

Seen in many voices
Been through many choices

Hard as an exception
bad as perception

Jungle mist

Dust of vehicles pass by
watch trees sway by
Fear not of dust hitting your eyes
hear out animal cries
Roaring of jungle mist
soaring of our interest folks insist
animals' outcome Jungle persists
humans' income taming of wild winds
to roll with dust while steaming
trucks roll with mist
Dust of vehicles pass by
as we watch trees sway by

Loyaly and cruelty

Loyalty precious element
Cruelty quality of nature
Chirping of birds
one feels wonderful about
the yelling of the wild that cries out

Cries of the wild
chirping of birds
both taking their fights
in their strides
cries of birds
chirping of wild
go hand in hand with
their strife's

Wonders of glance
seen from the house
keeping the stance
safe and sound
safe and sound stands
a chance when wonders of
glance are seen
from the house.

Memories

Every little thing
that human will have
always have memories

Check out a day where
There is something fun happening
It automatically would register in our minds

Memories can and
should be made only
at the time of fun and games
But they should be made always

Flip through the pages of a book
Write down the emotions that pass
through your brain
Write down your thoughts that you have

Cherish the albums
that you have
Reminiscences every moment
Of that time, you lived

Never ever think
these little moments
fade away
cause they actually last forever

Every little thing
that human beings have will
always have
memories

Monochrome

Colours of skin tones
don't matter at all

All that matters
is what is inside of the person

We need to decide if we want
to live in fear

Or do we want to live
as one united nation

Maybe we may think that
a darker person is more dangerous

But what makes us think that the
brighter folks are less dangerous

It's time we stop being kids and
start considering everyone as one nation

Let's reunite together and
merge together as a monochrome nation

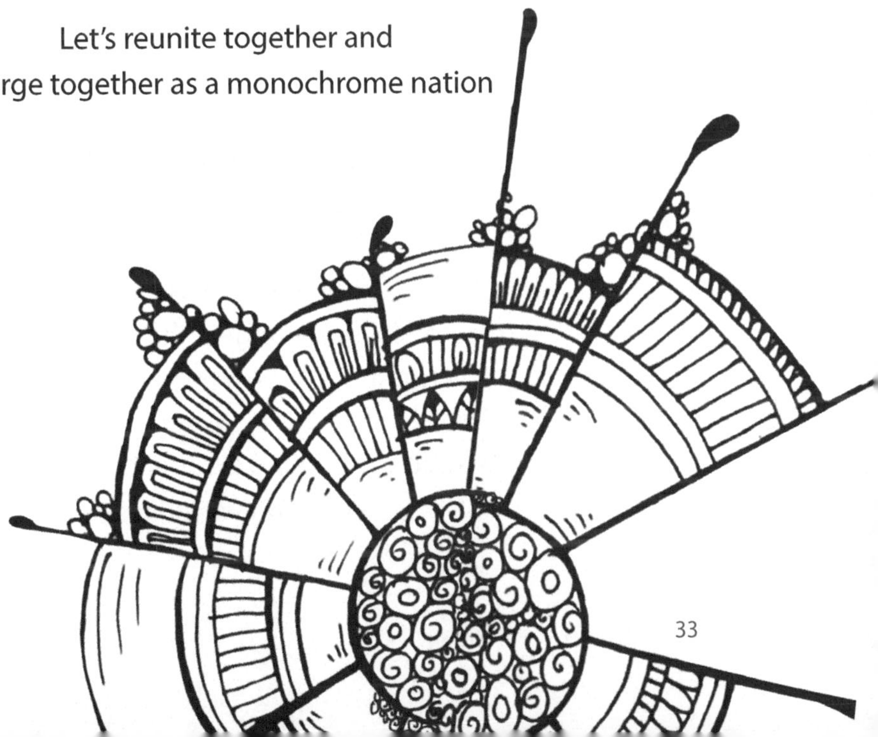

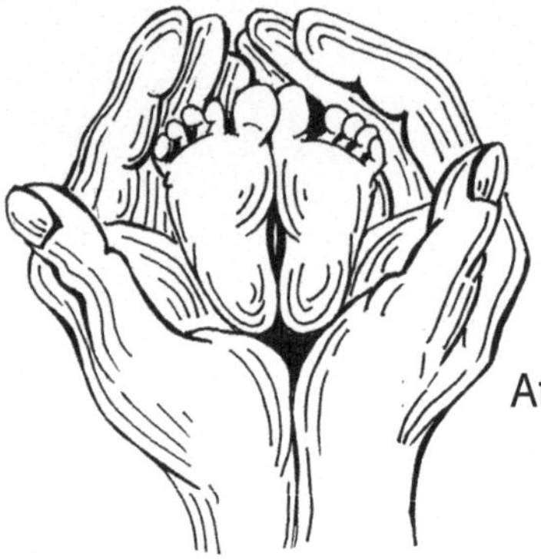

Mother's touch

Affection and being an affectionate person
this is what we all desired for

The authentic and warm heartened gesture
that is shown by
one very special human in all our lives

This angel has been sent from the heaven above
and yes, we call her mother

The pain the sacrifice and the sorrow
the joy the happiness and the success that we receive
is because of the unsung work that the angel has put in

She may be strict at times
but it's for the goodness of our mentality

The unsung work that every individual's angel
has to go through to get their entire life to
be what they are today

Angels keep doing what you do
and keep being the person you are

Every tiny creature that is
created by these angels should reciprocate
the humblest touch and the hero's love

Affection and being an affectionate person
is something we all desire for

People

Many a time there are
Many tribes that are unwanted in life

Many of the individuals will always push you into stuff
that may mortify your soul

Many a time it may be hard for you to cope
with the type of pain, you go through

Objections that people make can also hurt you
like a bullet in your chest

Don't ever let people around you
Take you for a ride

Don't ever let people around you
Try and push words inside you

Always love yourself
And then the relationship will flow.

Many a time there are
Many tribes that are unwanted in life

Many of the individuals will always push you into stuff
that may mortify your soul.

Race

What is life
if one may have a race
What will be life
if none may have to face their biggest summons
that arouse through their ways

What is life
if one may have to taste bitterness of fate
What will be life
if someone had to trace silver linings through their days
that showed on their face

What is life
if blacked out on some days, hacked out on items that pays
What will be life
if cracked out by the rays of sunshine
on the days that aren't bound to have lines with the numbers nine

What is life
if the whole globe started spinning on its axis
just for one to cope up with trees been cut with axes
What will be life
if the countries decided to part their ways just at times when it was 'bout to fade

What is life
if stone deaf to be heard by someone that would paint out a canvas
What will be life
if phones were deaf for a heard of none
to faint out of a canvas

What is life
if cyclones and thunderstorms arise for which individuals may
must add spice to the cries
What will be life
if typhoons and hurricanes occurred in parts of our space.

Reflections

Imaginations may run wild like horses without their reins
Individuals also can run wild
in imaginations like hearing noises of rains

What would be a beautiful sight
Just to see the conquering for fame
when one may see the sparks of flames

Scars of dwelling jewels may be left
for legacies to come in forms
that may not have been seen by one

Opening of horizons
with skies swelled with colours
that would never been seen by some

Mirrors of imagery that tickle one's sight
just for photography with lenses
that's not so bright

Flawless moments that may make one's jaw drop
through the massive reflections
that would be priceless moments to some

Beauty of the skies that reflect the horizons
for which breeze creates its own designs
Beauty of birds that flies reflect the rainbow seen in one's eyes.

Rise of twilight

Way up high shines a bright light
in the skies of twilight

Rising moon emerges
As waves submerges

Beauty of night skies
shine like wild eyes

Soul of bodies

Eyes that talk
with beautiful emotion
Wisdom that flock
with bundles of notions

Deep down feelings
felt by one
Crept out feelings
felt by none

Connections of individuals
empowered by one
Through arts being
discovered on the run

Wonders lie in
horizons
Mother's smile
with grins

Endeavors of individual's
through adventures
Endeavors of humans
That captures

Doors in life may close
Eyes in life may dose
Souls forever
soars

Struggles

Pain for some
effort for none

Fighting for survival
blending with revivals

Sometimes hard to achieve
something's hard to receive

Pain seen in eyes of one
as others see fun

Hardships faced by many never quitting
hardships faced by many never retiring

Struggles one goes through seen as desolation
snuggles one comes throughseen as inspiration

Pain for one
effort dies numb

Truth

Never run away from the truth
As it can lead to misunderstanding

Never say you did
Not do something as it can lead to sadness

You can run away from yourself
by not telling the truth

But if you run away from the sake of being scared
You would cheat yourself

Truth is a good thing to say but only follow the truth
And the rest will follow automatically

Truth brings us to life in everything
We do and we say

Vast horisons

Colours are like fireworks
They may sometimes just dwell with the skies

These colours can create a beautiful horizon that may
sometimes be hard to catch by our eyes

Each layer of that time of sunsets come together to reunite
The vast horizons teach us to be open minded

Velvet beauty

Colors of nature mesmerize one's eye
Colors that feature bird's fly

Wigs small, yet beautiful
Trees big, yet fruitful

Smooth flight of velvet
Smooth flight of beauty

Flight high mesmerized colors
Being shy phenomenal flower

Wildflowers

Uniqueness found rare
Openness found unfair

Blossoms out of mud
In paces unknown

Blooms out of sand
in spaces unknown

Discourages faced by few
Oh Lord, say 'phew'

Deep into soils dig minds that spoil
Crept into toils big kinds that foil

Taking flight like breeze
handling plight as freeze

Blooming petals, opening fatal
glowing with brightness, blossoming out darkness

Woman

Incredibly special
Yet super compassionate

Beauty of work
That's replicated
By very laddie
Surrounds wonders

Strongest treasures
That one could ever picture
Through every
Lady endeavors, new adventures

Strengthen bonds
Keep growing every aspect of life
Strong emotions throughout life

Incredible special
Yet super compassionate
Creating beauty
Like new worlds
Of wonders

Acknowledgments

Publishing my thoughts has been a dream that has been initiated, nurtured and supported by so many

I specifically want to thank

God: for giving me the ability to express myself through poetry.

My Parents: for understanding my emotions and supporting my intention to share these thoughts with a wider audience.

Both my grandmothers: for their unconditional love and for keeping me smiling and making me stronger person.

My Friends: for your patience, for being my fellow travelers and most importantly, believing in me. Love you guys loads.

Last but not the least I would love to thank my mentors for making me believe that anything and everything is possible and can be achieved.